Muwa
The Arch Enemy of the Empath

Totukani Amen II

Inner Alchemy's Publishing
Chicago, IL

First Edition

ISBN 978-1-949432-03-9

Any trade names, trademarks, service marks, etc., mentioned in this publication are for identification only. Therefore, any specific company or product mentioned is owned by their respective owner and not by Inner Alchemy's Publishing. Further, the company or product mentioned neither owns, endorses, nor has heard of Inner Alchemy's Publishing.
By stating this, we can avoid printing the ®, ™, ©, etc. marks that we might otherwise have to place throughout the text.

The publisher does not participate in, endorse, or have any authority or responsibility concerning private business transactions between our authors and the public.

Published by:
Inner Alchemy's Publishing, Inc.
332 S. Michigan Ave.
Ste 121-C141
Chicago, IL 60604-4434

info@inneralchemys.com
www.inneralchemys.com

Printed in the United States of America

Contents of Letter

Disclaimer

*All information contained within this title is
for entertainment purposes only.*

*The author or publisher assumes no responsibility from what one
may do with the information contained herein.*

*The content of this document should be read or viewed
and utilized as a work of fiction.*

Acknowledgements

I meditate and pray that those of you on the path who have embraced the way, that your load is light and your connection to the creator grows ever stronger.

Introduction

As I write this we're currently in the Month of October during the year 2020. It has been a interesting year with the entire world's economy being slowed and in some markets brought to a complete halt.

It would seem to many that this was some random unforeseen event. Maybe even to others a force of God punishing the wicked but in-fact it was just the carrying out of a plan (phase 1) to usher in a new age.

In the beginning of this year countries started to close their borders, travel became restricted and the populace of earth was ordered to not leave their homes.

We did not close our doors.

We were not put in a state of worry.

Nor were those who stayed in tune with us on the path (the way) filled with worry.

This and more are what we've been meditating on, and strengthening our internal selves, preparing, watchful.

As such we received a massive amount of calls asking will we be closing down or canceling our spiritual events and retreats?
Will we not be shipping the 'life saving' supplies across the planet?
Of course we are here and we did not close our doors and we shipped thousands of parcels across the planet. People also joined in from faraway places of earth to commune together. And the prayers and meditations that have been felt from across time and

space make this journey through the ups and downs of this reality well worth it.

More than anything else we thank you for staying in tune with us for whatever your need may be. It is in-fact the reason we're here. The fact why at most of our events, conferences and telephone based conversations the importance of 'the way' is stressed and how one should adhere to certain simple practices incorporated into their everyday life as it will not only prepare one for what is unknown, but it would bring one closer to that which cannot be explained via the tongue.

Which leads us to this material herein that gives yet another piece into the 'muwa' (pronounced, moo-wa) its ways, practices, strengths and weaknesses. So rather you're a neophyte (beginner) or adept (master) on this path, one could benefit from the ever watchfulness of another so that your travels may be uneventful and your internal state at peace.

There is nothing like when one's peace is broken.

As there have been countless Masters who have come before, and countless Masters who will come after. From both sides of the aisle (Left hand/Right hand paths) all dropping in to this sacred brew their essence which will bring about the singularity, oneness.

I implore you to come out to one of our live events where we teach sacred spiritual and mental techniques of defense, ancient form of martial art of Mind and Spirit. If this is being read at a time where this no longer is happening or far into the future where the teacher is no longer here in the flesh, seek out the books written and those that have learned the ways and can teach the techniques as they have been taught to them.

Even though Dr. Delbert Blair did not like the term of Master, because we're all in an ever state of learning. Accepting this 'ever state' when Master Blair ascended to dwell within the Temple of the Creator, many Master's across the realm gathered and asked with the permission of the one who sits on Mount High, would I do the honor to continue on teaching others in the way, which would elevate Master Blair to Grand Master in the heavenly plain.

This has nothing to do with the day to day running of the Center as that was already being done and had been going on for a while even when Dr. Blair was still here in the flesh. 3rd dimensional life is just that, 3rd dimensional and not difficult nor something that I think much of since I was doing the exact same things a decade before.

This was a spiritual based role that I personally steered away from all my life because in being gifted with the sight, I already knew what was in store for humanity. How many would take the path toward the Creator, and the majority of those that will defy and muddy the path to bring the collective consciousness downward because of being Muwa. And the wasted energies and time that would be spent repeating the same scriptures over, hoping enough not only hear, but listen.

In this place there is something called destiny, paths that lead toward a specific destination, and this destination has a seat that has your name on it. As such, when communing with the creator, and accepting the role, it elevated Master Blair to Grand Master as a Master was created after him, of a lineage of teaching which is ancient, and has been shared over a uncountable amount of time, by an uncountable amount of Masters.

All taking part in this cosmic theater.

If I were to summarize Grand Master Blair's entire catalog of teaching into one phrase that is so simple to understand yet immensely profound. One phrase that he has stated time and again which was:

"There is no truth, until you decide what Truth is."

And may the Grand Master be at peace forever inside and outside of time.

Empath

First, what is an empath?

Let's define empath utilizing popular online search results which states:

An empath doesn't just feel for someone — they feel with someone. Taking in others' emotions so deeply can make you want to do something about them.

So an empath is someone who is able to bring internally the emotional state of another. These states could be of happiness or sadness and could in many cases cause distress upon the empath if one does not know how to guards one's heart and mind (see, Book-I Lessons).

Many times empaths are feeling emotional states that did not originate from themselves, but instead from a person, people, or community that surrounds them. As such, pure empaths are able to more readily understand the emotional nuances of those that suffer and if balanced, able to ascertain the cause of the issue.

Who can be an empath?

Empaths can be:

- Male or Female
- Tall or Short
- Young or Old
- Rich or Poor
- Lighter Skinned or Darker
- Be of any ethnicity

- Be of any racial group
- Be from any country
- Have any educational level

As the above examples show, an empath can be anyone and the reason this was stated like this, is so one understands that judgments or better yet bias can cause ones perception to become cloudy which leads to potential mistakes or travesty taking place.

If I had to put a percentage on it I would say less than 20% of humans are pure empaths while over 50% of humans have some type of empathic like quality.
This number is a presumption of course based on the data of social dynamics of countries which includes social programs and the response to tyranny and strife that the populace shows.

If we were to equate empathic concentration to a diluted drink. A pure empath would have zero dilution, this would be a drink of full strength. While anything less than full strength would of course have varying degrees of dilution.

As such certain natural and common human qualities should not be confused with being an empath. As even the Muwa can show these qualities.

Examples:

- How one feels concerning a person, place or thing
- How one feels concerning circumstances or events
- How one feels internally concerning self

Empathic abilities should not also be confused with physic abilities which one could have one, or both.

Another common misconception is one being highly sensitive or emotional, being equated to one being empathic. This is again not so, one could be a highly sensitive person and yet not be empathic at all.

What are some of the pros of an empath:

- *Relates to humanity on a level that goes deeper than flesh*
- *Typically puts the interest of another before self*
- *Tends to look for employment that can have some sort of community/social uplifting and becomes a major bonus if it pays well*
- *Tends to be the one who people come to for advice*
- *The empathetic ability is the main attribute within the attributes of humanity that can detect the Muwa*
- *If balanced, tend to be phenomenal at being a parent since they understand the nuances children may show without words to describe inward feelings*
- *Pure empaths can sense, see and at times even smell the muwa*

What are some of the cons of an empath:

- *The Muwa being the predator's that they're, manipulate the empath with guilt knowing the empaths nature*
- *Since the Muwa seeks out positions of power, they will use this power to destroy or highly limit the empath since the empath is the only one who can see thru their grand standing, silver tongued words and false narratives put forth*
- *If the empath does not know their limit and stick to it, this is used by the Muwa to scam, or take more than their share which at times leads to forms of abuse*
- *Empaths are often passed up for managerial roles*
- *The Muwa can sense, see and at times even smell the empath*
- *The Muwa and its cohorts target the empath knowing the empath more than likely will not fight back. This targeting could be in physical altercations or slander*

Being an empath does not mean being nice nor a push over. Even though the Muwa thinks of empaths in this manner does not mean it to be so. Empaths are in many positions in this world in-

cluding warriors, heads of companies, military generals, presidents and the list goes on. In the current dynamic they're far and few between since those roles specifically attract a type of entity that will fight to the brutal end to obtain it and in many cases it just isn't that serious and quite burdensome for most empaths to pursue.

A power word for the empath is 'No'.

Because empaths will tend to over exert themselves helping others one needs to know truly what their limit is and stay balanced within. When one tries to take you outside of that balance, the answer is simply no. The Muwa will try, and they will push and potentially even punish you because you won't allow them to abuse you.

The Empath is literally the only barrier stopping the Muwa from destroying everything.

The Muwa

First, what is a Sociopath?

Let's define sociopath utilizing popular online search results which states:

A person with a personality disorder manifesting itself in extreme antisocial attitudes and behavior and a lack of conscience.

In many circles it is discussed and theorized that sociopaths are more so created by their environment and not necessarily born. An example of an environment that could create such an individual is one that everyone is out for themselves. As such, the children are usually the first neglected which in turn potential creates another generation of sociopaths since they had to look after their own needs since those who were supposed to provide and protect them did not.

Also,

Let's define psychopathy utilizing popular online search results which states:

Psychopathy, sometimes considered synonymous with sociopathy, is traditionally a personality disorder characterized by persistent antisocial behavior, impaired empathy and remorse, and bold, disinhibited, and egotistical traits.

In many circles it is discussed and theorized that psychopaths are more so born than created by their environment.

It is also theorized that many if not most heads of powerful positions, rather they be companies, governmental, military, etc., are all full of psychopaths since they're usually the first to, or naturally drawn to positions which gives them control over others and praise. Bonus points if it gives both. Extra bonus points if the societal control structures do not maintain the checks and balances that keep these types from going overboard. If they do go overboard watch out, since it will likely lead to overt, sadistic actions not only privately but publicly.

As a modern day example, there is nothing wrong with being in front of the camera especially if it is your business to do such. But these types would always be in front of the camera, always wanting you to look at them and to praise them. A tip to train your ability is when you're watching your favorite personality on YouTube, Facebook, or other social networks, is the presenter acting as normal human would no matter what the subject may be? Or are they actually trying to sway your emotions by acting out certain activities in front of the camera to purposely create a connection so you will move one way or another? So you will buy this or protest that. So you will look in this direction while they move a bit closer behind you without you noticing.

In the business world they would call this marketing. The ability to change or sway ones thought processes one way or another by means of subtlety. To invoke certain internal emotional states which in reality is just slyness, witchery.

A pied piper of shadow (Learn the techniques of the 'Witch & the Oracle' taught at the center).

From this point on we will call the sociopath/psychopath the Muwa unless we need to explain specifics to differentiate between the two.

Who can be the Muwa?

Muwa can be:

- Male or Female
- Tall or Short

- *Young or Old*
- *Rich or Poor*
- *Lighter Skinned or Darker*
- *Be of any ethnicity*
- *Be of any racial group*
- *Be from any country*
- *Have any educational level*

As the above examples show, Muwa can be anyone and the reason this was stated like this, is so one understands that judgments or better yet bias can cause ones perception to become cloudy which leads to potential mistakes or travesty taking place. Especially with the aforementioned personality types since they're always plotting on how they can be above you in whatever environment that you may coexist.

It is theorized that the Muwa seek power, status, fame, attention like how a person feels hunger. An insatiable drive toward these pursuits but let's not mistake the Muwa for a person who just likes to be in front of the camera. This is where the technique of nuance come into play as one is able to pick up on the signs (Learn the techniques of 'Nuance', taught at the center).

In the current world Muwa behavior is encouraged by all means, from the catering of one group over another, or because the corporate bodies modus operadi is to make profit by any means. Mysteriously those within these corporate structures, this body, operate all of a sudden without humanity, poisoning drinking water, earth, air, and setting ablaze the flora and fauna.

Muwa may seem something as simple as the aforementioned, being caused by environmental factors and/or genetic predisposition. From a third dimensional perspective this may be true but it is indeed a spiritual infliction. The conundrum is, is this a spiritual infliction caused by the downward trajectory of humanity or is thee infliction causing the downward trajectory itself because of their nature? The Chicken or the Egg, which came first?

What are some of the pros of the Muwa?

- *Tend to have little to no fear*
- *Bold*
- *High self esteem*
- *Lack of empathy which is great in war*

Because of the lack of fear, plus being bold with a high self-esteem, they're able to manipulate others into acts that may benefit a community, company, or regiment.

What are some of the cons of the Muwa

- *Manipulative*
- *Lacks Empathy*
- *Impulsive*
- *Aggressive*
- *Arrogance*
- *Egotistical*

A power word for the Muwa is 'to control, power'.

An example of this is doing anything it takes to make you 'believe'. So if it takes to look and smell like a millionaire bucks then that is what it will be. Or, if it means to have long hair in locks (dreads) saying keywords like consciousness, wearing crystals while taking photos of them eating fruit, and yelling to the world that they're vegan to get you to believe... well that's an option too.

Each of the aforementioned cons in itself could be a book. But the main takeaway that I would like you to know is that when you come in contact with these types they in more cases then not, are associating with you because of an underlying reason. It is just not to be lovers, friends, after work buddies, or even a client. More times then not they've an interior motive and unless you take heed to the signs, you will not know this until fire and brimstone is raining down. Their arrogance betrays them more times than not because unfortunately for them, in thinking of you in some substandard way assume you will not notice nor understand the reasons of them being around. They believe themselves to be so smart, so intelligent, so cunning, that it is no way you would know what they're up to until it's too late.

They believed themselves to be so intelligent, so cunning, so untouchable, that their arrogance manifested into them calling themselves principalities; Gods & Demons. So to emphasize how untouchable they're making them as if they're the foundation of this reality like Air, Earth, Water & Fire. But they're not. These are stories to tell the lower classes to make them fell powerless against the might of Muwa.

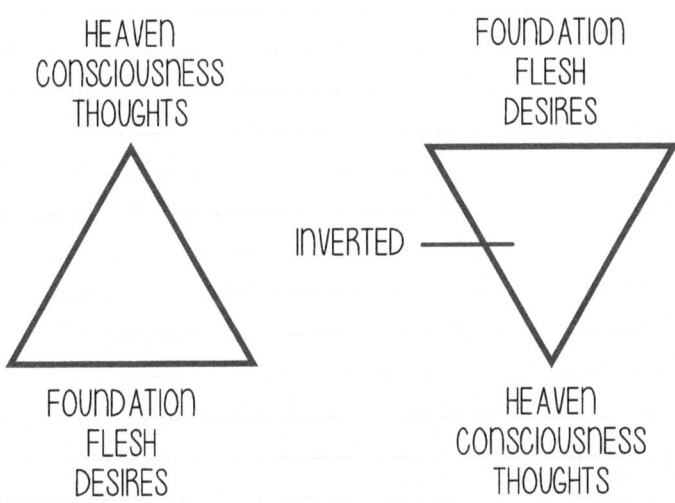

When an empath denies a Muwa's advancement they invert, which leads to its destructive tendencies showing which will be unleashed on you or anyone close to you.

Thru our studies we have seen this inversion cause a fracturing of the mind which leads to them talking to themselves, various personality splits to acts of violence against self or others.

Just as the there are pure empaths, there're also pure Muwa, and then varying dilutions of it. Currently in the world of 2020 via the Gregorian calendar there is an overabundance of Muwa in various dilutions within the population, overly-saturated.

Remember, the Muwa needs attention, status and power just as you need to breath. As such they are typically the first to volunteer to be a leader. As this is seen in most if not all movements including the 'New Age' a.k.a. 'Awakened'.

The reason for this is based on the knowledge of knowing the fundamental role of most in society. This role for most, is to follow, for better or worse. We're currently in a time where everyone is told they can lead, and everyone wants to be the one on the podium but in reality the majority are followers, that is their prime directive. This is evident by what they think, and what they say, which is in most cases just a regurgitation of what they have heard someone else say on the internet, TV, radio, or in their social circles. Also the need for leaders in movements (even though there is an ancient reason why this is needed and it is indeed needed), and to pray to gods. This is stated not to make fun of anyone, nor make one feel substandard, but just to give a 100% dose of what reality actually is.

Can you handle the dosage?

As such, the empath and Muwa both are aware of this even if it is on a subconscious level which is part of what is taught in some mystery schools, especially those of the left hand path to control society. Because they understand the fundamental nature of those in society.

The Muwa is an actor of emotion.

The one thing about the current age and social media is that you can see all types of phenomenon out in the open, public, for all to see and examine. One of these acts of emotion is have you ever seen an adult just be told no, or something doesn't go their way, and they just burst out crying? They're so immensely upset, so much so that they have an emotional breakdown, but yet there's no tears, there's nothing that is actually of real pain, except the whining and acting as if they're crying? Have you ever seen this?

Have you ever seen someone tell what seems to be a joke and everyone does this fake laugh? Now this doesn't mean the people who do this (which is quite common) are Muwa. But why are you 'acting' a laugh and not actually laughing? Because it is not funny, which means you shouldn't laugh. So why fake it and do that huff-puff fake laugh that is 100% fake?

The Muwa is an actor of emotion.

And in these acts no matter how ridiculous they are trying to sway the internal state of those who're observing. They're clicking franticly on the button labeled 'prime directive' which is one of the few key directives inside all human beings on earth.

Are there other prime directives? Of course, but that subject is for private classes and training since there are many who should not know these truths because they will only use them to manipulate and cause even more turbulence within peaceful spaces.

Lastly, do not allow bias or pre-programmed perception to deceive you. Most of these types are not walking around looking like something from a nightmare. But instead, they wear nice clothes, rather it be a suit or a dress. They smell good rather it be the scents of Issy Myake or whipped Shea butter.

"Do not give what is holy to the dogs; nor cast your pearls before swine, lest they trample them under their feet, and turn and tear you in pieces"
(Matthew Chapter 7, Verse 6)

#pretendyourhuman

The Pestilence

The standard definition of pestilence via merriam-webster.com is:

1: a contagious or infectious epidemic disease that is virulent and devastating especially: BUBONIC PLAGUE

2: something that is destructive or pernicious

One of the most common uses, or what one may refer to when they say 'pestilence' is referencing the bubonic plague. One of the so called most deadly instances of this in human history is 1347-1351 and killed approximately 75-200 million people.

The reason for giving an explanation of the above was to only use as a reference to show the word pestilence in use and to give a definition thereof.
One can easily see that it is a extremely serious and weighted word and brings with it terror, death, and disgust.

There is something much deeper than the 3rd dimensional explanation of this word. When I hear the word pestilence it's so weighted in my mind's eye beyond something of flesh. Something so weighted that it penetrates the flesh and leaks into the soul. This is the true pestilence and is what has penetrated the soul of humanity and has been causing the series of woes that many experience. And these series of woe's separate them from being in the know concerning their creation, creator, and why they're here in the first place.

In the movie Star War's there's a famous quote by Yoda that goes:

"Fear is the path to the dark side... fear leads to anger... anger leads to hate... hate leads to suffering.

So it all starts with the first piece which is fear. Fear in itself may seem like a simple emotion, and nothing to worry about, but within a person it festers... grows and leads in the end to suffering.

The same is with the Muwa. Their traits, taken independently may not seem as bad or something to worry about, but it festers... grows and leads in the end to suffering.

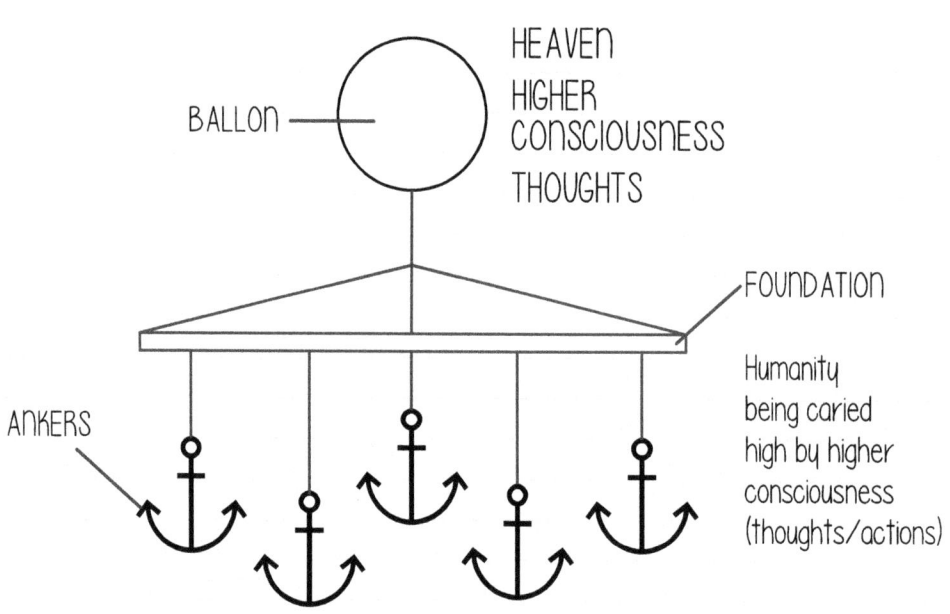

BALLON

HEAVEN
HIGHER
CONSCIOUSNESS
THOUGHTS

FOUNDATION

Humanity
being caried
high by higher
consciousness
(thoughts/actions)

ANKERS

Those of Muwa, and others who bring humanity
downward via witchery, evil, sin, selfisness etc.

As the above picture shows, the Muwa and those that serve it over time bring reality downward. A way to picture is reality is as a floating platform which is floating via a huge balloon that represents higher consciousness. This balloon (air) is tied to this foundation (earth) and all dwell on this foundation. Ideally if those on the foundation are not waited down by Muwa, evil deeds, etc., the balloon will continue to take the mind's eye upward, closer to the Creator. But when more deeds are done that oppose this higher consciousness it attaches anchors to this foundation bringing it downward. Think of it like cosmic crabs in a barrel metaphor.

There are no secrets in this reality. Many try to hide them, especially the Muwa, but indeed they can only for a time. As long as the consciousness is growing, eventually all is brought back into full clarity well past 720p into 8k clarity.

As you probably have already summated that the pestilence and the Muwa are practically one in the same. The Muwa are inflicted with a disease of spirit that is highly infectious and the only protection against it seeping within your heart is to live within your heart (see, Book-I Lessons), guard your mind and limit the uptake of this disease by righteous actions.

It's not about being perfect which is especially what a Muwa would think from the previous passage. But it's about 'ever-perfecting' the self. Forever growing like the great ginormous trees that reached the heavens and seeded the entire planet before they were cut down.

Stand up, plant your feet on solid ground, and look up to the heaven's and know, without any doubts that the Creator shines its warmth upon your face and gives you also the cold nights so you may see what the absence of the love may be. So that you..., will know without a doubt what is true and not by the words spoken by those who follow the way, that there is a place beyond the sickness and death, and the choice is yours with every waking breath as your life is flashed before your eyes, and the choices you made when given a chance to choose.

Do you think it is by pure happen stance you're reading this ob-
scure book? That as I'm typing this I'm thinking of you is just a fairy
tale? And those changes that would happen within your personal
life which would reflect in the external world around you are something I'm just wasting my time here writing about? What is spoken,
its ancient origins, told by many of the way, are the remedy to all.

Lastly, and most importantly the reason why the reality around us
wants everyone to fit inside a mold. Wants you to act like, dress
like, everyone around you is because then you become predict-
able, knowable. The Muwa since they lack actual human emotions
as if they're alien to this realm; knowing that humans are capable
of so much it's just much easier to contain them within a box. So
over time, all the uniqueness of humanity is slowly taken away.
A modern day example is by creating policies, laws, which end
up squeezing out all the unique shops, restaurants and theaters
within a geographical area which only leave the Muwa's estab-
lishments. Which are typically of low quality, overly saturated and
without humanity.

And with that, until our next correspondence,

Be well.
Master Amen

ADDITIONAL WORKS
BY AUTHOR

An Alchemist Journey in Scent
Author's Life Story

ADDITIONAL WORKS
BY AUTHOR

Book I–Lessons
Karma Release and Internal Power Generation

ADDITIONAL WORKS
BY AUTHOR

Compression
A Neophytes Guide to the
Mystical Energies of North and South America

ADDITIONAL WORKS
BY AUTHOR

Sacrament of the Forest
How to become a Guardian of the Forest

ADDITIONAL WORKS
BY AUTHOR

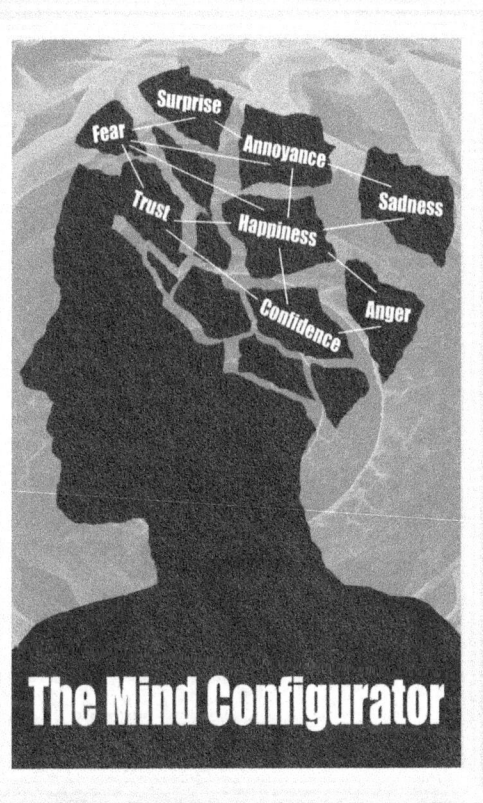

The Mind Configurator
Advanced Technique to access the Subconscious Mind

ADDITIONAL WORKS
BY AUTHOR

2020
Quantum Clarity within the Conscious Collective

ADDITIONAL WORKS
BY AUTHOR

The Sacramentum
Tarot/Oracle Cards

Notes

Notes

Notes

Lightning Source UK Ltd.
Milton Keynes UK
UKHW020659080321
379980UK00015B/1754